BOOK TWO

DRUM CLASS METHOD

by Alyn J. Heim

FOREWORD

This is a method for the drum class. It effectively presents the rudiments of drumming and the reading of music in a manner and at a pace designed to accommodate the specific needs of group instruction.

Each technique or rudiment is introduced by a rote <u>Drill</u>, developed through a reading <u>Exercise</u>, and refined by a <u>Solo</u> performance that stimulates interest and challenges each member of the group.

This new method contains fresh ideas that will be welcomed by the class drum teacher. In Book I the "free-bounce" approach to rolls is introduced and developed with explanations to both teacher and student. A full section is devoted to six-eight time using a method that enables the student to learn the rhythm "in-two" from the beginning.   Book II begins with sixteenth notes and progresses to some of the more advanced rudiments and reading materials. More than half of each book is devoted to appealing solo material which is designed to develop the student by encouraging enthusiastic practice.

About the author: Dr. Heim received his Bachelor of Science degree from the Juilliard School of Music where he majored in tympani and percussion under Saul Goodman. His Master of Arts degree in Music Education was earned at Columbia Teachers College, and his Doctorate in Music Education at New York University. He is a former member of the Houston Symphony Orchestra and a music teacher and supervisor in the public schools of New Jersey.

Solo Page

Eighth and Sixteenths

Solo Page

Paradiddle

DRILL

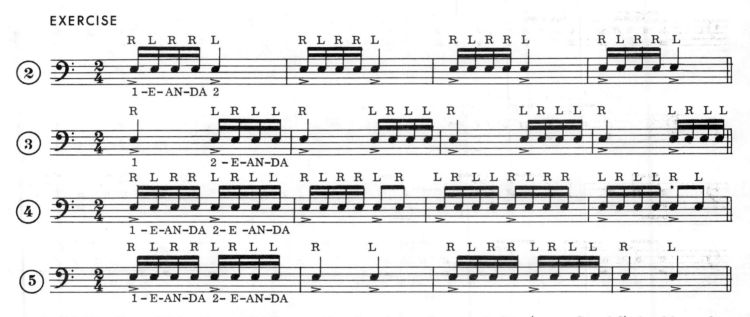

The first stroke of each paradiddle should be accented. Since the accent needs height to be effective the preparatory lift is made as indicated by the arrow. Be sure that the unaccented strokes are soft and as close to the drum or pad as possible. As speed develops the double stroke becomes a bounce.

EXERCISE

IMPORTANT: For additional paradiddle practice the sixteenth note studies (pages 2 and 3) should now be practiced using paradiddles for each four sixteenths.

Double Stroke Sixteenths

The following figures are often played with a double stroke at very fast tempos. As speed develops the double stroke becomes a bounce.

IMPORTANT: For additional practice the studies on pages 4 and 5 should now be played with a double stroke supplied on the sixteenths.

Solo Page

Paradiddle Duet

Five Stroke Roll on Eighth Note

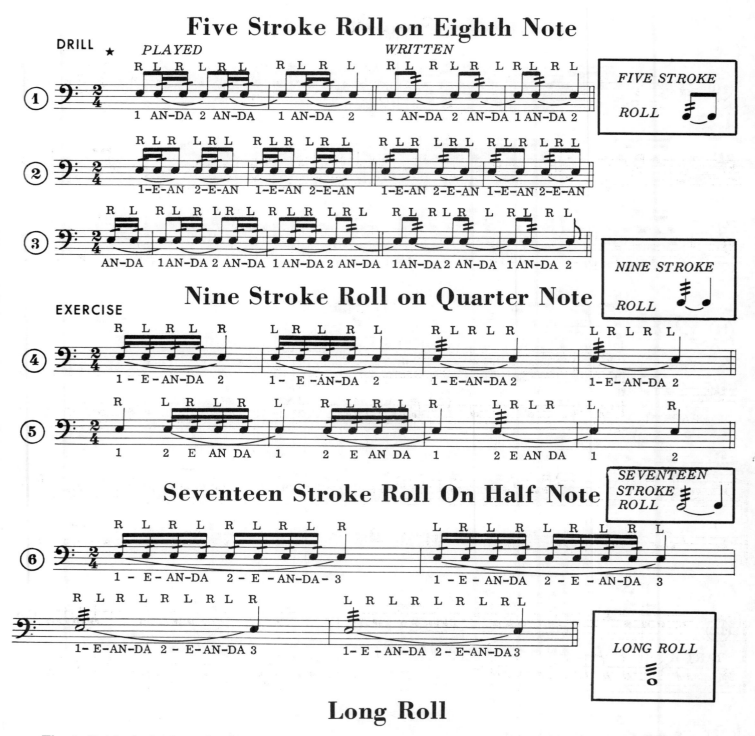

Nine Stroke Roll on Quarter Note

Seventeen Stroke Roll On Half Note

Long Roll

The individual strokes of a long roll are not counted. A good sounding roll is produced at a comfortable speed and is continued for the correct number of counts. The beats of the roll need not fit in with the tempo of the count.

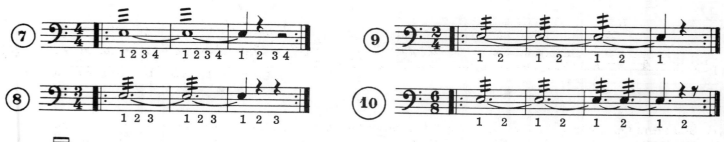

★ ♪♪ – Bounce strokes are fully explained on page 11 of Book I.

Roll Solo Page

Conclusion Solos - Section I
Fanfare

High Step

Drumology

To Coda

D. C. al Coda

Coda

Solo Flight

E. L. 1336

Cut-Time

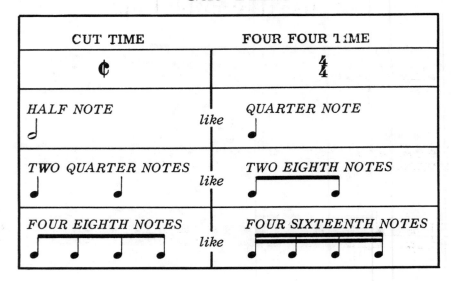

CUT TIME		FOUR FOUR TIME
¢		$\frac{4}{4}$
HALF NOTE	*like*	*QUARTER NOTE*
TWO QUARTER NOTES	*like*	*TWO EIGHTH NOTES*
FOUR EIGHTH NOTES	*like*	*FOUR SIXTEENTH NOTES*

EXERCISE

Cut-Time Solo Page

Rolls In Cut-Time

E. L. 1336

Cut-Time Roll Solo Page

Duet

Dotted Eighths and Sixteenths

This rhythm is simple to imitate. After the teacher has introduced the count the student can easily perform the exercises even though he may not fully comprehend the notation at this stage.

Solo and Duet Page

Duet

PART I

⑭

PART II

Double Paradiddle

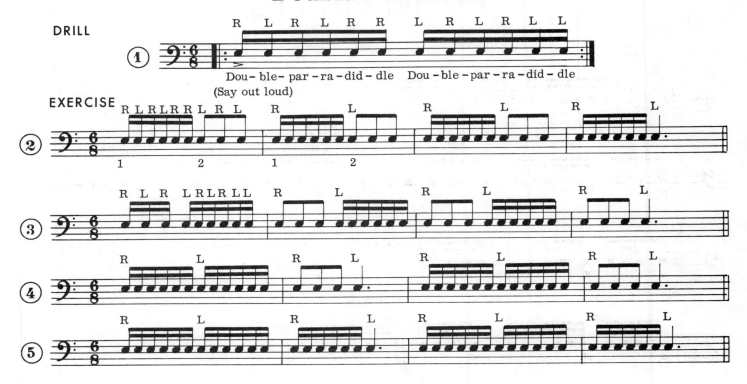

Double Stroke Sixteenth

E. L. 1336

Solo and Duet Page

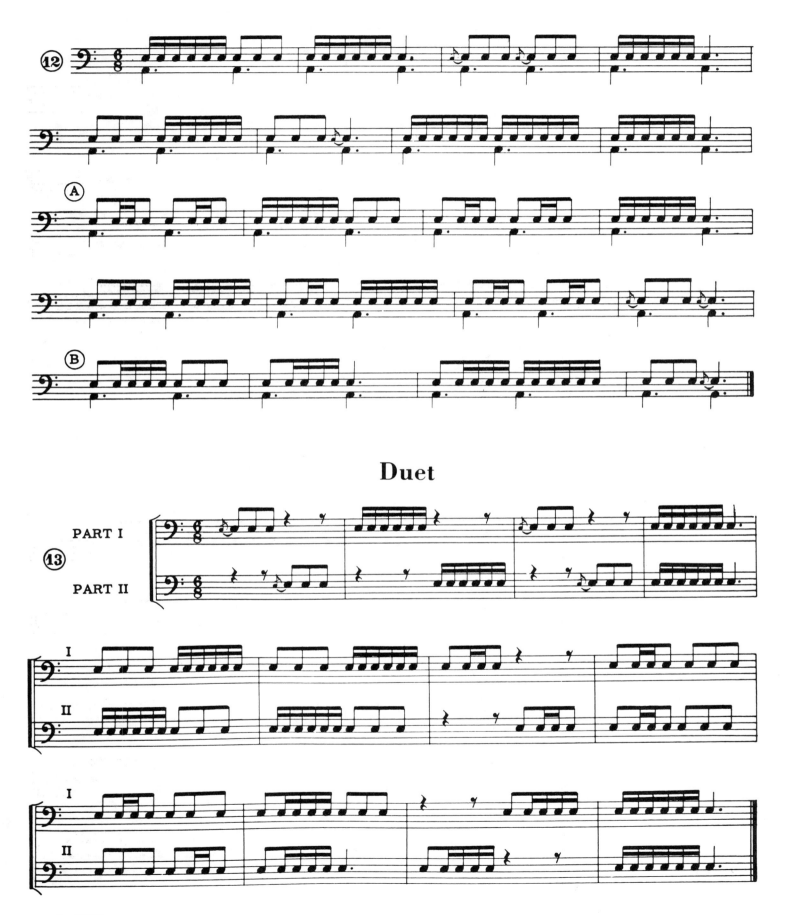

Duet

Conclusion Solos - Section II
Drummer's Delight

Double Tap-A-Diddle

Two Snares In Cut-Time

Flams On Sixteenths

DRILL

EXERCISE

IMPORTANT: The student should now play the solo's on page 23 before going on to the Flamadiddle.

Flam A Diddle

DRILL

EXERCISE

IMPORTANT: The solo's on page 23 can now be played again, this time using a Flamadiddle for each group of four sixteenth notes.

Solo Page

The added accent gives the Flamacue its character.   After this rudiment has been drilled, the above solo can be played once again using a Flamacue for each group or four sixteenth notes.

Flamacue

IMPORTANT: For additional practice, pages 2 and 3 can be played adding a Flam, Flamadiddle, or Flamacue for each group of four sixteenth notes.

Ruff (closed drag)

DRILL

The hand positions for a Ruff are the same as for a Flam. The Grace note in a Ruff is a crushed bounce stroke; this being the only difference between the two rudiments.

EXERCISE

Alternating Ruffs

DRILL

EXERCISE

E. L. 1336

Solo Page

Duet

Open Drag

Since the Open-Drag and Ratamacue are among the most difficult rudiments to perform they are not given full presentation in this book.   The more advanced students will find the above speed studies helpful in preparing for these rudiments.

E. L. 1336

Successive Rolls
(not tied)

This roll is most effectively produced by both sticks playing a crushed bounce stroke at the same time.

Solo Page

E. L. 1336

Accent Studies

Right Hand Accents

DRILL

Accents need sharp contrast to be effective, therefore the un-accented notes should be played very soft.

EXERCISE

Right and Left Hand Accents

DRILL

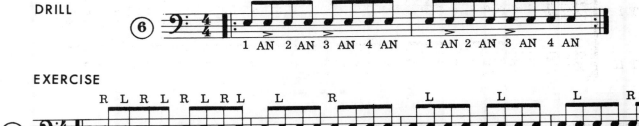

EXERCISE

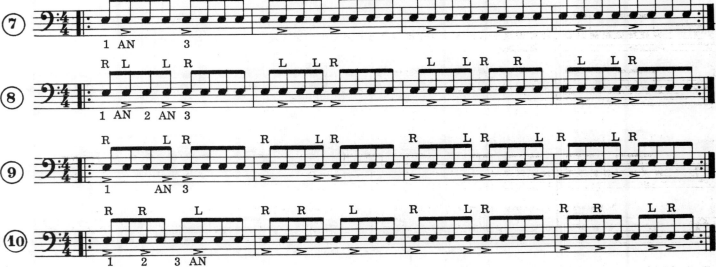

E. L. 1336

Solo Page

DUET

Conclusion Solos-Section III
Sound Off

Street Beats

Two - four

Accented Two - four

Six - eight

Accented Six - eight

Duet Finale